Pieces of Vincent

by David Watson

First performed at Arcola Theatre on 2 September 2010

Arcola Theatre is funded by the Arts Council England

Supported by
**ARTS COUNCIL
ENGLAND**

Arcola Theatre and Pieces Productions present

Pieces of Vincent

by David Watson

Cast

VINCENT CAIRNS	Adam Best
RACHEL WILSON	Sian Clifford
MARGARET CAYLEY	Tricia Kelly
JOHN CAYLEY	Kevin McMonagle
KHALID MASAUDI	Charles Mnene
ANNE O'CONNELL	Dearbhla Molloy
CHRISTOPHER KABILA	Joseph Rowe
DENNIS KESSNER	Robin Soans
AMAR SALEEM	Shane Zaza

Production Team

Director	Clare Lizzimore
Set Design	Es Devlin
Costume Design	Signe Beckmann
Lighting	Peter Mumford
Sound	Ian Dickinson
Design Associate	Bronia Housman
Design Assistants	Cordelia Chisolm, Suzannah Lombardelli
Casting	Lotte Hines
Production Manager	Finbar Cahill
Stage Manager	Ruth Murfitt
Props	Martha Mamo
Assistant Stage Manager	Latoya Lewis

Film Team

Film Maker	Daniel Lang
Cameraman	Andreas Bergmann
Video Consultant	Sam Pattinson
AV Project Manager for XL	Chris Ferrante

Producers	Leyla Nazli for Arcola Theatre Clare Lizzimore and David Watson for Pieces Productions
Press	Jennifer Reynolds for Target Live (020 3372 0950)
Production Photography	Simon Annand
Rehearsal Photography	Robert Workman

arcola
theatre

Over the last ten years Arcola Theatre has taken thousands of theatregoers on a theatrical journey by producing and presenting some of the most diverse and challenging work on the London stage. We have presented plays and opera that have rarely seen the light of day as well as revisiting more contemporary playwrights and presenting the finest international work. Arcola has championed new writers and emerging directors and offered a continuing platform on which to continue their journey. Alongside this we have built a thriving youth and community programme and pioneered sustainability in the arts.

For Arcola Theatre

Artistic Director	Mehmet Ergen
Executive Producer	Leyla Nazli
Executive Director	Ben Todd
General Manager	Catherine Thornborrow

Youth and Community Projects

Youth & Community Projects Manager	Owen Calvert-Lyons
Youth & Community Projects Co-ordinator	Nicola Hatton
Youth & Community Assistant	Phillippa Augustin

Sustainability

Sustainability Projects Manager	Feimatta Conteh
Sustainability Projects Assistant	Tom Morris
Marketing Assistant – Fuel Cell	Amanda Warnick
Associate Technologist	Matthew Venn

Marketing

Marketing Manager	Barry Wilson
Marketing Assistants	Selvi Akyildiz, Venessa Howell, Aaron Robb

Production

Technical Manager	David Salter
Venue Technician	Hilary Williamson
Technical Assistants	Nicola Maddox
	David Todd

Finance

Finance Manager	Helen Hillman
Finance Assistant	Amanda Koch-Schick

Front of House and Box Office

FOH Managers	Charlotte Croft, Shane Fitzgerald, Harriet Warnock
Duty Manager	Amanda McLaren
Box Office Assistant	Tim Blackwell
Bar Supervisor	Haydar Koyel
Bar Staff	Pauline Hoare

With thanks to all our dedicated volunteers and interns

Pieces Productions

Pieces Productions is committed to finding and producing astonishing but overlooked new plays. It has been established in order to allow a new wave of work to be seen on British stages. The company aims to support new contemporary writers whose plays are politically and socially engaged, and adventurous in form.

For Pieces Productions
Artistic Director   Clare Lizzimore
Co-Artistic Director   David Watson
General Manager   Chris James

Thank you to

Sir Alan Ayckbourn, Mike Bartlett, Caryl Churchill, Central School of Speech and Drama, Dominic Cooke, Gabi Dempsey, Elyse Dodgson MBE, David Eldridge, Mike Figgis, Michael Frayn CBE, Mark Goddard, James Grieve, Ramin Gray, Robert Holman, Sean Holmes, Sir Nicholas Hytner, Mel Kenyon, Phyllida Lloyd CBE, Duncan Macmillan, Ric Mountjoy, Alan Rickman, Ian Rickson, Sir Tom Stoppard OM, CBE, FRSL, Rachel Taylor, Lyndsey Turner, Victoria Walsh, Richard Wilson OBE, Effie Woods, George Perrin, The Peggy Ramsay Foundation, Tara Wilkinson, Simon Stephens and everyone at XL Video for their generous support of this production.

AV kindly donated by XL Video

Cast Biographies

Adam Best (Vincent Cairns)

Adam studied at the Royal Welsh College of Music and Drama. His theatre credits include: *By the Bog of Cats* (Wyndhams Theatre), *Truckstop* (Company of Angels), *On a Starless Night* (Roundhouse, Camden), *Journey's End* (Original Theatre Company, National Tour).

His film and television credits include: *Silent Witness, Holby City, Waking the Dead* (BBC), *The Catherine Tate Show* (Tiger Aspect), *The Bill* (Talkback Thames), *Cup Cake* (Wee Buns Productions/Northern Ireland Screen), *Blooded* (Magma Pictures).

Adam's radio credits include: *John Walker's Blues* (BBC).

Sian Clifford (Rachel Wilson)

Sian trained at RADA and is a founding member of THE ORDER.

Theatre Credits include: *The Road to Mecca* (Arcola Theatre), *Pains of Youth* (National Theatre), *Is Everyone OK?* (Nabokov Tour), *Parthenogenesis* (Royal Opera House), *Public Displays of Affection* (Nabokov at Latitude), *The Pendulum* (Jermyn Street Theatre), *Burial at Thebes* (Barbican & Tour), *Not The End Of The World* (Bristol Old Vic), *Listening Out* (BiteSized for the Royal Court), *Contractions* (Theatre 503 for the Royal Court), *Without Laughing* (Practicum Theatre).

Film Credits Include: *The Other Me* (Rebelmonk Films).

In the autumn, Sian will return to the National Theatre to play Beauty in Katie Mitchell's production of *Beauty and the Beast*.

Tricia Kelly (Margaret Cayley)

Theatre credits include: *This Wide Night* (Bernie Grant Arts Centre), *Blue Heaven* (Finborough Theatre), *The Adventures of Nicholas Nickleby* (Gielgud/Chichester/Toronto), *Some Explicit Polaroids* (Out Of Joint), *Julius Caesar, Ion* (RSC), *The Maths Tutor* (Hampstead Theatre), *The Inland Sea* (Wilton's Music Hall), *Local* (Theatre Upstairs), *Juno & the Paycock* (National Theatre), *King Lear* (Hackney Empire), *Amphytryon* (Gate Theatre), *The House under the Stars, The Way of The World, The Choice* (Orange Tree Theatre), *Venus & Lucrece* (Almeida Theatre). Wrestling School credits include: *Victory* (Greenwich), *Seven Lears, Golgo, The Last Supper* (Royal Court), Joint Stock/Royal Court credits: *Fen* (also New York), *A Mouthful of Birds, Deadlines, When We Are Married* (West Yorkshire Playhouse/Liverpool), *Unprotected* (Everyman Theatre/ Traverse – Amnesty Award), *The Seagull, Government Inspector, As You Like It* (Crucible), *Dancing at Lughnasa* (Salisbury).

TV & Film credits include: *Eastenders, My Family, Casualty, The Bill, High Stakes, In Sickness and In Health, Cristobel, Dangerous Lady, A Small Dance, Top Dog, Real Lies.*

Kevin McMonagle (John Cayley)

Kevin's theatre work includes: *The Unconquered* (Stellar Quines at Arcola Theatre), *Black Snow, Resistible Rise of Arturo Ui, Further Than The Furthest Thing* (National Theatre), *Richard III* (RSC), *Family Reunion* (Donmar Warehouse), *Ambulance, Karate Billy, Thyestes, Ladybird* (Royal Court Theatre), *Wishbones, Heartthrob* (Bush Theatre), *A Message for the Brokenhearted* (BAC), *Russian National Mail* (Sputnik at Red Lion & Ekaterinburg Festival), *Hamlet, Broken Glass* (West Yorkshire Playhouse), *Cat & Mouse[Sheep]* (L'Odeon), *Woyceck, Fall, Girls of Slender Means* (Edinburgh Fringe), *Educating Agnes, Waiting for Godot, The Plough and The Stars* (Citizens Theatre).

Television credits include: *Krakatoa, Quite Ugly One Morning, Bramwell, Your Cheatin' Heart, The Long Roads, Blue Murder, Rebus, Morse.*

Charles Mnene (Khalid Masaudi)

Charles' theatre credits include: *Pandora's Box* (Almeida Theatre), *Sing Your Heart Out For the Lads* (Theatre Royal York & Tour), *The Bolt Hole, 59 Cups* (Birmingham Rep), *Miller's Tale* and *The Pardonner's Tale* (whilst at Kingsway College).

Charles' film credits include: *New Town Killers, Games Men Play, Leaving Eva, Fallout, Jew Boy, Life in Lyrics, Birds Eye View, Chromophobia* and leads in both *The Great Ecstasy of Robert Carmichael* and *The Train Game.*

Television credits include: *Misfits, Casualty, Dubplate Drama, Silent Witness, Shoot the Messenger, Dream Team, The Bill, Holby City, Undercover, Ahead of the Class, Doctors, The Chosen One.*

Dearbhla Molloy (Anne O'Connell)

Theatre includes: *In Celebration, Arcadia, Hamlet* (West End), *On the Ledge, Hinterland, Cripple of Inishmaan* (National Theatre), *The Hostage, Shadow of a Gunman* (RSC), *Ditch* (Old Vic Tunnels), *Plough and the Stars* (Young Vic), *Juno & the Paycock* (Donmar), *Doubt* (Tricycle), *Summerfolk, Saturday Sunday Monday* (Chichester), *Dancing at Lughnasa, Juno & the Paycock, Touch of the Poet* (Broadway), *Cripple of Inishmaan* (Atlantic Theater, New York).

TV includes: *Wallander, U B Dead, Touch of Frost, Last Detective, Waking the Dead, Foyle's War, Midsomer Murders, Coronation Street, 55 Degrees North, Stan, Sex and the City, GBH, The Fragile Heart.*

Film includes: *The Damned United, Blackwater Lightship, Home for Xmas, Tara Road, Bloom, Run of the Country.*

Awards: Drama Desk Award (2), Theatre World Special Award, London Critics Award, Irish Theatre Award (2), US Audie Award. Nominations: Tony Award, Irish Film and Television Award, Royal Television Society Award, Grammy Award.

Dearbhla is an Associate Artist of the Abbey Theatre, the National Theatre of Ireland.

Joseph Rowe (Christopher Kabila)

Joseph is a recent graduate of The Birmingham School of Acting.

Theatre credits include: *Macbeth* (Broadway Theatre), *The Fear of Queer* (Birmingham Library Theatre), *Of Mice and Men* (Black Box Theatre Company), *The President of an Empty Room, A Midsummer Night's Dream, The American Clock* and *Three Sisters* (all Birmingham School of Acting).

Television credits include: *The Tower* (pilot from Uzong Films).

Film credits include: *The Lodger* (short film from Andrew Wickett Productions).

Robin Soans (Dennis Kessner)

Robin's theatre credits include: *The Rivals* (Southwark Playhouse), *On The Beach* and *Resilience* (Bush Theatre), *Coriolanus, Under the Black Flag* (Globe Theatre), *On Ego* (Soho Theatre), *The Holy Terror* (Duke of York), *Anything Goes, Loves Labours Lost* and *A Prayer for Owen Meany* (National Theatre), *Push Up* (Royal Court).

His film and television credits include: *Midsomer Murders* (Bentley Productions), *Waking the Dead, Dalziel & Pascoe, Jonathan Creek, Dangerfield* (BBC), *Miss Marple* (Granada), *Rebecca* (Carlton), *Inspector Morse* (Zenith), *The Last Hangman, The Queen* (Granada Pictures), *Not Only But Always* (Company Pictures), *Method* (Castel Pictures), *The God Club* (Little Fella Productions), *AKA* (Independent Dreams).

Shane Zaza (Amar Saleem)

Shane's theatre credits include: *The Ark* (Arcola Theatre), *Peter Pan* (Barbican/National Theatre of Scotland), *Macbeth, Romeo and Juliet* (Shakespeare's Globe), *Oxford Street* (Royal Court Theatre), *Macbeth, Players* (West Yorkshire Playhouse), *Deadeye* (Soho Theatre/Birmingham Rep), *Billy Liar* (Liverpool Playhouse), *Mercury Fur* (Menier Chocolate Factory), *George's Marvellous Medicine* (Bolton Octagon), *The Master and Margarita, Kes, The Arbitrary Adventures of an Accidental Terrorist, Nicholas Nickleby* (Lyric Hammersmith), *The Long Way Home* (New Perspectives), *East is East* (New Vic Theatre).

Television credits include: *Mouth To Mouth* (Avalon/BBC), *The Omid Djalili Show, Spooks, 10 Days To War, Casualty, Murphy's Law, Doctors, Dalziel and Pascoe, Waterloo Road, Messiah, Watch Over Me* (BBC), *The Bill* (Talkback Thames Television).

Film includes: *Love@1stSight* (1st Sight Films), *The Da Vinci Code* (Columbia Pictures and Imagine Entertainment).

Radio includes: *Bora Bistrah, Orwell's Babies* (BBC).

Production Team Biographies

David Watson (Writer)

David's first play *Just a Bloke* was staged as part of the Royal Court's Young Writers Festival when he was 17. Other plays include *Flight Path* (Bush Theatre/Out of Joint) and *Any Which Way*, performed by ex-offenders for Only Connect Theatre Company. He has written short plays for the Birmingham Rep and Tricycle Theatres, and is currently Writer in Residence at the Lyric Hammersmith. His TV work includes *L8R* (Hi8us/BBC), for which he won a Children's BAFTA.

Clare Lizzimore (Director)

Clare Lizzimore is an award winning theatre director. Her credits include *Faces in the Crowd* by Leo Butler (Royal Court Theatre), *War and Peace, Fear and Misery* by Mark Ravenhill (Royal Court Theatre and Latitude Festival), *On the Rocks* by Amy Rosenthal (Hampstead Theatre), *Jonah and Otto* by Robert Holman (Royal Exchange Theatre, Manchester), *Tom Fool* by Franz Xaver Kroetz (Glasgow Citizens Theatre and Bush Theatre – Nominated for four CATS Awards), *The Most Humane Way to Kill A Lobster* by Duncan Macmillan (Theatre 503) and as Co-Director with Max Stafford Clark, *The Mother* by Mark Ravenhill (Royal Court Theatre). Clare has also directed new plays from Russia, Nigeria, Portugal and Romania, and travelled extensively for the Royal Court Theatre's International Programme, developing new plays with artists in Africa and The Middle East. Her awards include the Channel 4 Theatre Directors Award 2005/06 and the Arts Foundation Theatre Directing Fellowship 2009. She is currently Creative Director of Clean Break Theatre company, for whom she will curate and direct *Charged* - a season of six new plays to be presented in association with Soho Theatre in November 2010.

Clare is the new Associate Director at Hampstead Theatre.

Es Devlin (Set Designer)

Es trained at Bristol University, Central St Martins and Motley. Opera designs include: *Salome* (Royal Opera House), *Carmen* (ENO), *Gadaffi* (ENO), *Knight Crew* (Glyndebourne), *Faust* (Dresden SemperOper*)*, *I Puritani* (Netherlands Opera), *La Clemenza di Tito* (Liceu, Barcelona), *Don Giovanni, Flammen* and *Macbeth* (Theater an der Wien), *A Midsummer Night's Dream, Billy Budd* (Hamburg), *Jeanne D'Arc au Boucher* (Accademia Santa Cecilia, Rome), *Orphee* (Linbury), *Powder Her Face* (Ystad, Sweden).

Theatre designs include productions for RSC, National Theatre, Royal Court, Almeida, West End and Broadway.

Dance collaborations include: Russell Maliphant, Anthony Van Laast, Rambert, Cullberg and Northern Ballet Theatre.

Concert designs include Lady Gaga, Muse, Goldfrapp, Take That, Kanye West, Pet Shop Boys, Imogen Heap, Nitin Sawhney and Mika.

Forthcoming engagements include *Die Tote Stadt* (Helsinki), *Lucrezia Borgia* (ENO), *Les Troyens* (ROH) *Parsifal* and *The Cunning Little Vixen* (Copenhagen), MTV Europe Music Awards and *Batman* for the O2 Arena.

Awards include the Linbury Prize for Stage Design (1996), TMA Best Design (1998), Olivier Award for Best Costume Design (2006) and TPI Stage Designer of the Year (2010).

Signe Beckmann (Costume Designer)

Signe is from Denmark, Copenhagen and trained at the Danish Design School and at the Motley Theatre Design Course.

Theatre credits include: *Dr. Faustus* (Watford Palace Theatre), *House of Bernarda Alba, Dealer's Choice* (Embassy Theatre), *Ghosts* (Young Vic), *About Tommy* (Southwark Playhouse), *Dancing at Lughnasa* (Aubade Hall, Japan), *Scenes from an Execution* (Hackney Empire), *Pedro and the Captain* (Arcola), *Love In Idleness* (Bristol Old Vic), *Breaking News* (Theatre 503).

Her opera credits include: *La Serva Padrona* (Sá de Miranda, Portugal), *Volume* (ENO Opera Works), *Eugene Onegin, Giasone* (Iford).

Dance credits include: *Meridian, Phantasy* (Rambert, Queen Elisabeth Hall).

Signe was also stylist on *Kate Moss Liberation* (Liberation Magazine).

Peter Mumford (Lighting)

Recent theatre credits include: *The Misanthrope, Prick Up Your Ears* (Comedy Theatre), *A Midsummer Night's Dream, Miss Julie, Bedroom Farce* (Rose Theatre), *A View From The Bridge* (Duke of York's Theatre), *Pictures From An Exhibition* (Young Vic), *Parlour Song, Cloud Nine* (Almeida Theatre), *All's Well That Ends Well, Exiles, The Reporter* (National Theatre), *Carousel, Fiddler On The Roof* (Savoy), *Hamlet, Brand, Macbeth* (RSC), *Private Lives* (West End/Broadway), *The Seagull* (Royal Court Theatre/ Broadway) *Dying City* (Set/lighting Royal Court).

Opera and dance credits include: *Carmen, Madame Butterfly, Peter Grimes, 125th Gala* (Metropolitan Opera, NYC), *Take Five, E=MC^2* (Birmingham Royal Ballet), *Blue Beard's Castle, Punch and Judy* (English National Opera), *Petrushka, Carmen* also set design, *Cheating, Lying, Stealing* (Scottish Ballet), *Il Trovatore* (Paris), *Siegfried, Götterdämmerung, Fidelio, Don Giovanni, Two Widows* (Scottish Opera), *Eugene Onegin, The Bartered Bride* (Royal Opera House).

www.petermumford.info

Ian Dickinson (Sound - for Autograph)

Having previously been resident at the Royal Court Theatre where he designed in excess of fifty shows, Ian joined the Autograph design team in 2009. Autograph are a leading British sound design and equipment hire company.

Ian's most recent designs include: *After the Dance, Women Beware Women, All's Well that Ends Well* (National Theatre), *Spur Of The Moment* (Royal Court Theatre), *Jerusalem* (Royal Court Theatre & West End, Olivier Nomination), *Mrs Klein* (Almeida Theatre), *The Misanthrope* (Comedy Theatre), *1984* (Royal Exchange) and *The Rise And Fall of Little Voice* (Vaudeville).

Ian's first sound design in London was *Crime & Punishment in Dalston* at Arcola Theatre.

Bronia Housman (Associate Designer)

Bronia trained at the Motley Theatre Design Course and Kent University.

Recent designs include: *A Real Humane Person Who Cares and All That* (Arcola Theatre), *Sports et Divertessements/ Babar* (la Carrière de Normandoux) *Precious Bane, Sexual Neuroses of Our Parents, Shoot, Get Treasure, Repeat, Don Juan Comes Back From The War, The Laramie Project, Loveplay* (Arts Educational School) *The Execution of Damiens, Three short plays from Africa* (Momentum Festival, Nottingham), *The Promise* (New Wimbledon Studio), *Cosi Fan Tutte* (Classical Opera Company), *After Miss Julie* (Nottingham Playhouse), *For One Night Only* (Pleasance Theatre, London).

Recent work as Associate Designer to Es Devlin includes: *Blaze* (Touring) *Knight Crew* (Glyndebourne), *Take That, The Circus* (UK Stadium Tour), *I Puritani* (De Nederlandse Opera & Greek National Opera) *Pet Shop Boys Pandemonium* (World Tour).

Finbar Cahill (Production Manager)

Finbar graduated from Goldsmiths College and cut his teeth on the London fringe, originally specialising in sound, before joining the stage and aerial teams at the Millennium Dome. Then, in the West End, he spent many years as a resident technician (in venues such as the Strand, Comedy, Phoenix and Arts Theatres where he ended his tenure as Technical Manager). He returned to large venue work as Logistics Manager for the installation of the sound system in Wembley National Stadium before moving to Barcelona and becoming involved in experimental film-making. Finbar currently works in theatre and video production.

Ruth Murfitt (Stage Manager)

Ruth studied Stage Management at the Royal Welsh College of Music and Drama, professional theatre credits include: *Through a Glass Darkly, Slung Low* (Almeida Theatre), *Disconnect, Aunt Dan and Lemon, A Miracle, Faces in the Crowd, The Vertical Hour* (Royal Court Theatre), *Treasure Island, Miss Julie* (Rose Theatre, Kingston), *Puss in Boots* (Theatre Royal, Bury St Edmunds), *Free Outgoing* (The Royal Court Theatre & Traverse Theatre, Edinburgh), *Mickey Salberg's Crystal Ballroom Dance Band* (West Berkshire Playhouse, Newbury and UK tour).

Daniel Lang (Filmmaker)

Daniel was born in 1977 and raised in a British-German artist's family in Bavaria, he lived in Australia between 1986 and 1989, and from 1998 to 2001 he studied Film and Drama at the University of Reading. From 2001 to 2007 he was a directing student at the Film and Television School Konrad Wolf in Potsdam-Babelsberg, followed by a one-year stay in Beijing.

His short film *female/male* was awarded the German Short Film Prize in Gold 2005. His short film *Dog* had its premiere at the 56th Berlin Film Festival and was nominated for the German Short Film Prize 2006.

Daniel Lang lives and works in Murnau am Staffelsee and Berlin.

Sam Pattinson (Video Consultant)

Sam studied Sculpture at Central St Martins College of Art and Design, having produced for Vegetable Vision and United Visual Artists Sam went on to co-found onedotzero industries with Shane RJ Walter. He has produced the video content and design for *U2 Vertigo Tour* 2005 and *360 Tour 2010, George Michael 25 Live Tour 2006, The Rolling Stones 40 Licks Tour* 2002 and *Bigger Bang Tour 2005, Lady Gaga Monster Ball Tour 2009* and *The Pet Shop Boys Pandemonium Tour 2008.*

He produces for the following show designers: Willie Williams, Es Devlin, Kim Gavin, Patrick Woodroffe, Martin Phillips and Mark Fisher.

David Watson
Pieces of Vincent

faber and faber

First published in 2010
by Faber and Faber Ltd
74–77 Great Russell Street
London WC1B 3DA

Typeset by Country Setting, Kingsdown, Kent CT14 8ES
Printed in England by CPI Bookmarque, Croydon, Surrey

A CIP record for this book
is available from the British Library

ISBN 978-0-571-27361-4

2 4 6 8 10 9 7 5 3 1

For Noel Greig
late and still great

Characters

John Cayley

Dennis Kessner

Christopher Kabila

Rachel Wilson

Vincent Cairns

Amar Saleem

Khalid Masaudi

Anne O'Connell

Margaret Cayley

The play takes place now, but the scenes
do not happen in chronological order.

PIECES OF VINCENT

ONE

August.

County Down, in the shadow of the Mourne Mountains.
John Cayley. He is sixty-five. He is an Inspector with
the Police Service of Northern Ireland.

John On the eighteenth of August 1979 a man came.
Wee Ford Cortina.

Came up the pass, and he drove down.

And he painted the valley.

Saw dark reds, browns.

'Daddy, why does your man sit there all day with his
paintbrush and his paints?' I said, 'I don't know, had you
better ask him?'

In the nights, he came to an old barn. Old farmers'
place. Set up in there. Brought him out food, something
to drink. Didn't know his name. Didn't care to ask.

'Daddy, I saw the painting man, coming out the barn
this morning. Gave us a go with his paintbrush and now
I've paint all over me hands, Da, look.'

'I'll be a painter now, Da. I'll paint the whole world.'

In 1984. Two young fellers came from Attical, one
night in the summer. Pair a' them boozed up and, running
wild through the valley on their motorbikes and the
ending of the evening came, with the burning down, of
the barn.

Lit the sky, up over Donard, St Johns.

Didn't take us long, the next day, tracking 'em. Half a
dozen old ones in the village, clucking away. Interview
room by twelve – criminal damage, trespass.

The three of us alone. 'What's the game now, lads?
Why d'you do it?'

Older one looked at me.

With a kind a' knowing, know-all, know-nothingness on his face.

'Sure if we told you that, you'd be 'fraid to look us in the eye.'

Now that, knocked me, I don't know why.

Thunder in the valley.

Hands shaking on the way home. Shoes off, up the stairs, thinking a' nothing, or trying.

Sitting in his room up there, the rain falling.

Posters on the walls, never touched.

Looking down.

He said, 'I'll paint the whole world, Dad.'

TWO

July.

A house in Tufnell Park, London.

It is raining heavily outside. Subdued thunder. From upstairs, a radio can be heard – a soaring opera.

A piano in one corner. An old-fashioned telephone, which is ringing.

The music stops.

Dennis Kessner enters, hurriedly. He is fifty-four. He is barefoot, and wears a white shirt, which is tucked in, and dark trousers. He is German, although he has lived in London since the 1960s. As he enters, he is re-tying a bandage around his wrist. He picks up the phone.

Dennis Hello, 4238.
Yes.
(*Surprised.*) Oh, Christopher. Oh, my goodness.
Yes. Yes, OK.
OK. Well, I'll come to the door.

The doorbell rings – a real bell.

(*Laughs.*) Oh well, you're here now, of course you're . . .

He puts the phone down and exits. We hear him open the front door.

(*Off.*) Ah!

Christopher (*off*) Oh Gosh.

Dennis (*re-entering*) Christopher, my goodness, you're soaking.

Christopher (*entering*) Yeah, it's quite raining.

Christopher is a young man of twenty-three, although his mental age is some years younger. He wears a black hoodie, under which is a T-shirt which is slightly too big for him, with jeans and unfashionable trainers. He has a faint Nigerian accent.

Dennis Oh terrible. Now look at this thing, you're wearing.

Christopher (*laughs*) OK.

Dennis (*taking it off*) This is not the type of thing to wear in the rain, at all.

Christopher No, it's too small.

Dennis (*taking it off*) Well, it's not waterproof. You see?

Christopher OK.

Dennis There we are. Now are your other clothes OK?

Christopher OK.

Dennis Because you can change into something, if you want.

Christopher laughs.

Yes?

Christopher No.

Dennis You're sure?

Christopher No.

Dennis OK. Well, I'll make you some tea. You silly boy. Would you like tea?

Christopher Have you got a, apple and cranberry juice?

Dennis Juice? Well, I have tea, or I have water, so . . .?

Christopher Oh. (*Laughs, softly.*)

Dennis Would you like a cup of tea?

Christopher Er, tea . . . cup of water, please.

Dennis (*exiting*) Water.

Christopher laughs. He whispers to himself.

Christopher (*whispering*) Water.

Dennis (*off*) Oh, you silly boy, because you really want to go out, and get wet like this?

Christopher Yeah, I like the rain.

Dennis (*re-entering*) Oh, you're crazy.

Christopher Yeah, I'm crazy.

Dennis Here we are. Well, you're lucky, to find me here at this time.

Christopher Yeah, I'm lucky.

Dennis Because I'm often out, really, a lot of the time.

Christopher Yeah, I didn't know, that you was here. If.

Dennis Well, you see Wednesdays, oh my goodness it's a very funny thing: on Wednesday afternoons I go to Kentish Town.

Christopher Yeah.

Dennis Because there's a woman who lives there who plays the viola.

Christopher OK.

Dennis OK? And, some time ago she decided that, she would like to have some accompaniment, on the piano, and, we were put in contact, and so, every Wednesday she telephones, and she says, 'Is it OK for you to come?' And I say 'Yes, yes, I will come,' and . . . you know this happens, like clockwork really, until every day, until today, and this is the first day where this morning she rang me up and she said, 'Oh Dennis.'

   Christopher laughs.

She said, 'Oh Dennis,' she said, 'I'm so sorry I'm so ill, today.' And I said, 'This is fine,' you know. 'Next week I will come.' 'Or tomorrow.' You know, I have plenty of other . . . So it's very strange for me, today, and, but sometimes, you know, you're expecting one thing, and then, but then . . . something else happens, and, it's wonderful, and, so here we are.

Christopher Yeah.

Dennis So it's a lucky thing.

Christopher Yeah, there's people in the road. (*Laughs, nervously.*)

   Beat.

Dennis People? Oh, the boys. Yes, they are there of course, they're always there just sitting there . . . Even in the rain.

Christopher Yeah, it's raining.

Dennis And they say such nasty things, to people, I don't know what it is they're saying most of the time. It's just gibberish, to me of course. (*He laughs.*) Have to . . . walk past them. But how are you? Young man?

Christopher laughs.

Because for a long time I haven't seen you, you're, you're hiding from me.

Christopher No, I'm not hiding. I just get, busy sometimes.

Dennis Well, they say a busy mind is a happy mind, they say.

Christopher Yeah. Happy, happy-go-lucky.

Dennis Happy-go-lucky?

Christopher laughs.

Yes?

Christopher leans over and tickles Dennis.

Oh no no no no, careful calm, calm.

Christopher sits back, laughing. A beat.

You get, excited.

Christopher Oh gosh.

Dennis We must start from calm.

Christopher Yeah.

Dennis You see? Or how can you play, your Chopin, or your Beethoven when you are very, a beanbag? Full of beans.

Christopher Yeah, I play them, sometimes.

Dennis Well, you're wonderful. When you're not excited. (*Laughs.*) You're wonderful when you're excited and you're even more wonderful when you're not excited, of course.

14

Christopher Yeah, you teach lessons.

Dennis I teach, I teach. Not as many as, sometimes but there's a girl, who comes, she's, she's a very shy girl. You know. She's very nice, but . . .

Christopher Yeah, Martin comes, down the stairs and, with the cello, sometimes.

Dennis (*laughs*) Well, Martin comes, Martin is not here.

Christopher OK.

Dennis Any more.

Christopher OK.

   Beat.

Dennis Which is a strange thing because it's very changed, since you were last here. Of course.

Christopher Yeah, Martin's gone now.

Dennis Well, Martin has gone away to work and . . . Of course he was going away anyway really because you know he's a silly person.

Christopher (*laughs*) Yeah.

Dennis He really is and . . . (*Indicates his bandage.*) This is how I have my, wrist, bruised now.

Christopher OK.

Dennis Because he's a very angry person sometimes and he throws things and . . . I said to him, I said, 'When you're in a good mood, and you're happy you're an angel.'

Christopher Yeah.

Dennis 'But when you're bad, and you're . . . feeling depressed, you are a devil.' (*Laughs.*) It's true, you know He's a devil really.

Christopher (*laughs*) Yeah.

A short pause.

Dennis Because you see when you are happy, and you're fine, then, everything is really is joined up. In the world.

Christopher Yeah, it's joined up.

Dennis But when you're . . . depressed and . . . (*Beat.*) Well, it's just bits and pieces, really.

Christopher Yeah, it's lucky.

Beat.

Dennis And it's difficult, for you to understand but. But look at you.

Christopher laughs.

You look so well, you're so handsome. Do you feel well?

Christopher Yeah, I feel well.

Dennis And you're living in Southgate now?

Christopher Yeah, Southgate.

Dennis Oh, it's a long way.

Christopher Yeah, it's a long way.

Dennis But you like it there?

Christopher Yeah, I like it there because, I like it there because, there are people there who are very friendly.

Dennis Oh lovely. Wonderful. And you still have your job, at the supermarket?

Christopher Yeah.

Dennis Wonderful. And what do you do there, you're still, when the people bring the shopping you put it on the . . .

Christopher Yeah – pip!

He mimes a supermarket conveyor belt, and imitates the pips of the barcode reader.

Dennis *(laughs)* Yes.

Christopher Pip!

Dennis Oh well, you're a clever boy.

Christopher Yeah. Man.

Dennis Well, yes. And. Do you like the people you work with?

Christopher Yeah, I like them except for, Mikayla.

Dennis OK.

Christopher Because she's sometimes . . . not nice to me.

Dennis And are you nice back to her?

Christopher *(laughs)* No. No.

Dennis Well, you should be.

Christopher laughs.

Because even when people are not nice to us we can still be nice to them, of course.

Christopher Yeah, thank you for helping me for . . . *(Beat. He laughs, nervously.)*

Dennis Go on.

Beat.

Christopher Thank you for helping me for, when I was growing up and, and now that I am, a man, I can come to say . . . thank you.

Dennis Oh . . .

Christopher laughs, embarrassed.

Oh you don't have to say . . . these things to me, really.

Christopher (*laughs*) I want to.

Dennis Well, it's so nice, to see you again.

Christopher Yeah, I want to.

Dennis And to see you're so well.

Christopher (*getting bag*) Yeah, I bring something for . . .
Yeah, I bring something for Sammy.

Dennis For Sammy?

Christopher Yeah, I bring her, a present for her.

*He produces a tin of cat food from his bag. He laughs,
nervously.*

Dennis Oh, my goodness, well. This is another thing that
happened, and . . . Because one day I came into the
house, and, all along this carpet here I can see dark . . .
blood . . .

Christopher Eeurgh.

Dennis I know, patches, and, so I thought, 'My God,'
you know, and I went up the stairs, and, Sammy was
there . . . in the bedroom, and . . . really she was in a
terrible way.

Christopher Oh no.

Dennis With . . . bleeding and . . . And of course Martin
said to me, he said, 'You know this is something that
someone has done. To her.' You know, a, some, terrible
person.

Christopher Oh no.

Dennis Well, yes, and, so straight away we took her to the vet and, they said 'Really there is nothing we can do, for her . . .'

Christopher Oh.

Beat.

Dennis And so it's a very sad thing, but. And so we gave her to the vet, and, she's gone now, but. Of course you miss her. (*Laughs.*) You wanted to see her . . .

Christopher Yeah, I brought this . . .

Christopher lets another twelve tins of cat food fall out of his bag.

Dennis Oh my word.

Christopher (*cursing himself*) Sugar.

Dennis Well, it's fine, Christopher, really, because I tell you there's a cat down the road who will have these. A lovely tabby cat. You know, she'll be very grateful, to you.

Christopher Yeah, I'll take them back.

Dennis Well you can take them back or you can leave them here, or . . .

Christopher starts to pack them away. He stops. Beat.

So it's very sad, really . . .

Christopher Yeah, it's really.

Beat. Christopher looks up at Dennis. Christopher is crying. He laughs, embarrassed, through his tears.

Dennis Oh. Oh, you mustn't be upset. You mustn't be upset. You know it's a sad thing, of course, but we remember her. Don't we?

Christopher Yeah.

Dennis And it's raining now but the rain will stop. And we can go out. And you have your job.

Christopher Yeah, I have.

Dennis Which you like. And it's the summer. (*Beat.*) Will you go away for the summer or you'll stay here?

Christopher Er. Don't know.

Dennis No? (*Beat.*) Well, you can stay here. (*Beat.*) Well there are so many things, aren't there, to think about.

Christopher Yeah, there's too much things.

Christopher laughs, nervously. A short pause.

Dennis Play me something. On the piano. (*Beat.*) A-ha? (*Beat.*) And this will be something for, to cheer us up. Do you think?

Beat. Christopher laughs.

Dennis And we can even say, Christopher, we can even say, that you're playing it for Sammy. Yes? (*Beat.*) What do you think?

Beat.

Christopher Yeah, I haven't played for . . . (*He laughs.*)

Dennis You haven't played for a long time?

Christopher (*laughs*) Oh gosh.

Dennis Well, it doesn't matter. You know no one will hear. Apart from the boys. They don't mind. We can close the window.

Christopher hesitates, laughing softly. Beat.

Christopher OK.

Dennis OK?

Christopher laughs, embarrassed.

Christopher Which, music?

Dennis Anything. Really. Would you like to play . . .
Chopin?

*Christopher laughs. A beat. He gets his phone out. He
fiddles with it briefly, then plays a piece of instrumental
grime music on it.*

Oh my goodness.

Christopher laughs, excitedly.

Oh turn it off, it's horrible.

He turns it off.

Horrible. For how long have you listened to this kind of
thing?

Christopher Er, about seven months or something like
that.

Beat.

Dennis Well, if you've found something you like you
must listen to it, really, it's . . .

Christopher laughs. Beat.

Are you going to play something now?

*Christopher collects himself. A short pause. He plays a
short piece on the piano. It is a bit rusty to start, but
it is obvious he has a real talent. Dennis listens.
Christopher finishes. A short pause. Christopher laughs.
He plays the last note again.*

Christopher C flat. (*He laughs.*)

Dennis wipes away a tear. Beat.

Dennis Wonderful. (*Beat.*) Are you going to play it, again or . . .

Christopher (*laughs*) No.

Beat.

Dennis It's really wonderful, to hear you . . .

Christopher laughs. He gives Dennis a hug. Dennis holds him. Christopher laughs. A pause. Dennis kisses Christopher. Beat. He stops. Christopher laughs, embarrassed. Dennis stands.

Well.

Beat.

And do your school . . . do you still see friends from . . . ? Oh, it's . . . the time, suddenly. Well I'm so stupid, I'm going swimming.

Christopher OK.

Dennis With a friend of mine.

Christopher Oh no.

Dennis I wish you'd called me, next time you must call me, because it's really very difficult.

Christopher Yeah, I'll call you.

Dennis (*getting his coat*) You must take your, thing here. Is it still raining now?

Christopher Yeah, it's raining.

Beat.

Dennis Oh. Well, thank you for coming.

Christopher Yeah, thank you for coming. But . . .

Christopher looks at him, he can't find the words. He laughs, nervously.

Dennis I'll see you soon.

Christopher Yeah. See you soon.

Dennis Good boy.

Beat.

Well. I'll show you to the –

They exit.

(*Off.*) – door.

Christopher (*off*) Yeah.

Dennis (*off*) Take care.

Christopher (*off*) Yeah, bye.

Dennis (*off*) Goodbye.

> *The front door closes. Dennis re-enters. He stands
> there. A short pause. He plays with his bandage. He
> closes the lid on the piano.*

THREE

July.
  *A portion of an open-plan office, on the top floor of a
building in Southwark, London.*
  *A big window, which is open, leads to a balcony area.
Rachel Wilson and Vincent Cairns have just entered.*
  *Rachel is twenty-eight and from Surrey. She wears
smart office clothes, and is carrying her ID card. Vincent
is also twenty-eight, and from Northern Ireland, although
his accent has been softened by the years he's spent in
southern England. He wears almost trendy charity shop
clothes, and is holding a carrier bag.*

Rachel But what are you doing *here*?

Vincent Well . . . (*Half-laughs.*) D'you mean that, in an existential –

Rachel (*moving to her computer*) Oh Christ.

Vincent Well, I saw your pub there, y'know, that's if you can call it a feckin pub, and er, is this your office?

Rachel It's – No, it's not, no, this is all a dream.

Vincent Is it really –

Rachel It is yeah –

Vincent This is very interesting, I do need to have a wee.

Rachel (*sighs*) You fucking cretin, if they're locked downstairs they'll be locked up here.

Vincent I'll do it out the window.

Rachel Vincent.

Vincent Rachel. Hold this.

Rachel Why don't you go down to the third fl— Oh fuck it, I give up.

Vincent It happens to be, an emergency, so . . .

Rachel I'll put the kettle on, shall I, while you –

Vincent Climb out of this . . .

Rachel – piss up against the wall of . . .

Vincent (*off*) The wall of . . .

Rachel The corporate . . . beastling.

Vincent (*off*) Very good. Did I call it that? Oh that's better.

Rachel You've brought some bottled cocktails.

Vincent (*off*) I brought some what? Oh yeah. Yeah, I think they're symptomatic of a wider . . . cultural . . .

24

Rachel Extraordinary.

Vincent reappears.

Vincent Oh, thank Christ for that. And all his lovely angels.

Rachel Vincent, why couldn't you meet me as we arranged, like normal people, in the Uppers / Bar.

Vincent Oh Jeez, I mean the 'Uppers Bar' for crying out lou— 'Upwardly mobile' it stands for, probably –

Rachel Oh ha ha / ha.

Vincent Oh ha ha ha, Rache I just think it looked a sort of fucking awful soulless hell.

Rachel I think it's nice.

Vincent Well, I think you think it's nice because you think you ought to think it's nice. Actually.

Rachel Oh, of course, I mean I'd probably fall down and die if I had the merest sniff of a . . . independent thought –

Vincent Well I remember a time when . . . opinion and . . . imagination were still on nodding terms. Or maybe I don't.

Rachel No.

Vincent Maybe I'm deluded.

Rachel Maybe we all are.

Vincent Maybe everything we think we've lost we never really . . . had. Rachel Louise Catherine . . . Wilson.

Rachel Hello.

Vincent Hello.

Beat.

Rachel Shall we start again?

Vincent Start what?

Rachel Life? Living?

Vincent Well, it's a nice day for it.

Rachel Well, it started off raining and now it's . . . sunny.

Vincent Oh, it's glorious.

Rachel I like the summer.

Vincent Yes, I do. I like the girls.

Rachel Of course.

Vincent I want to kiss their bottoms.

   Beat.

I'm so sorry.

Rachel No no.

Vincent You look gorgeous.

   Beat.

Rachel 'K you.

Vincent Who were you talking to?

Rachel What?

   Vincent mimes typing on a keyboard.

Oh, just . . . finishing off a few –

Vincent Him indoors. Checking up on you.

   Beat.

What a prick, who's he think he is?

Rachel Well, he's my husband –

Vincent And what have you done today? In what you might describe as . . . your life?

Beat.

Rachel Well, today I have been mostly . . . archiving.

Beat.

Vincent Uh-huh?

Beat.

Rachel On . . . cases going back to . . . oh, about ten years ago –

Vincent What do you mean by cases?

Beat.

Rachel Well, cases.

Beat.

Vincent Oh, right.

Beat.

Rachel And if the clients are liable to . . . pursue further work with us then they go in one file and if they aren't then they go in another.

Beat.

Vincent Sounds great.

Rachel half-laughs.

What?

Rachel (*quietly*) Fuck off.

Vincent No, I mean it, y'know I mean you sound . . . And that's quite a view you have there, no?

Rachel It's the River Thames.

Vincent And how much do you people earn?

Rachel (*laughs*) 'You people.'

Vincent Well, just you then.

Rachel Erm, about thirty K?

Vincent Well, that's pretty good.

Rachel Yes.

Vincent If you like that sort of thing.

Rachel Better than a punch in the face.

Vincent Yes. Which is coincidentally what I was on the . . . receiving end of, few nights back.

Rachel No way.

Vincent Yes way. Look at that. See?

He indicates a little scar.

Rachel But Vincent, who could possibly want to punch you?

Vincent Er, quite, well, a man, a person. On a bendy bus.

Rachel How did it feel?

Vincent Excellent, I enjoyed it.

Rachel I bet you did.

Vincent When I was at school, in posh school, I don't know if you remember I actually went to a rather less than prestigious boarding school in the south of England –

Rachel Yes, I do recall.

Vincent The older boys, used to stand in the doorways, of the dormitories, with their hands full of . . . pillow cases full of . . . snooker balls and God knows what else and they'd make the younger boys . . . run up and down the corridors and they'd shhhmack us on the legs as we're going past, bang, bang. Bang.

Rachel How horrible.

Vincent Yes. And marvellous somehow.

Rachel I wonder what it's like to be stabbed.

Vincent Well, stabbing was never on the agenda in my school, y'know. Good clean violence . . . was all. Big bruiser boys from Aldershot and . . . Camberwell. er Camberley. I'm nervous. D'you know? Why am I nervous?

Rachel I don't know. I think you probably know the answer more than I do.

Vincent I think it's maybe because I don't know how much you value me. Any more. D'you know what I mean by that?

Rachel What sort of a . . . question's that?

   Beat.

Vincent Months . . . pass y'know We don't speak to each other, I live in Dalston, you live in . . . Chipping Clegton. Y'know, anyone looking in, at us, from . . . outside would think . . . y'know?

Rachel Would think what?

Vincent (*sighs*) Oh . . .

Rachel Of course I va— What a stupid . . .

Vincent Yes it is a stu—. I thought you were gonna make us some tea.

Rachel I have done, it's there.

Vincent You have done, yeah, God knows what kind of . . . constituency it's in now . . .

Rachel (*laughs*) Constituency?

Vincent Let's . . .

Rachel Gosh, I didn't realise it was . . . political.

Vincent Let's, let's / just.

Rachel Vincent, why d'you feel you have to ask me if I value you / any more?

Vincent I don't know, it's just a stupid . . . where I'm at and . . .

   Beat.

Rachel (*the cocktails*) Or maybe we should have these instead.

Vincent Great, yeah, but let's just . . . stop. (*Beat.*) Because I've got something to . . .

   Beat.

Rachel What? (*Beat.*) What?

Vincent I'm er, I'm going to Australia, I'm going back to Australia.

   A short pause.

Rachel You're going . . .

   Vincent laughs.

Great. Wow. When are you . . . Oh well that's . . . When are you going?

Vincent Er, the fifteenth. Of the . . . August.

Rachel Wow.

Vincent Three weeks.

Rachel Oh my God.

Vincent I know.

Beat.

Rachel And are you happy, or are you nervous or . . .

Vincent Er, yeah, I'm happy yeah, I'm looking forward to seeing my mum. And my dad. And Jamie.

Rachel (*smiles*) Jamie.

Vincent Yeah, he's eighteen now.

Rachel God.

Vincent Yep.

Beat.

Rachel And do your parents still like it?

Vincent Not really, no, they're quite unhappy, er, in lots of ways.

Rachel Oh no.

Vincent Yeah. Yeah. Y'know, their business is . . . not gone the way they would have liked and . . . Yeah, I just think they're a bit lonely. Really. (*Beat.*) So, yeah, I'm happy and I'm nervous and . . . I should have told you.

Rachel Well.

Vincent Earlier.

Rachel Yes.

Beat.

Vincent Well I'm . . . telling . . . / telling you now.

Rachel Telling me now.

Vincent I'm telling you now, yeah.

Beat.

Rachel Well that's great news.

Beat.

Vincent Is it?

Beat.

Rachel Of course. Oh, I'm . . . pleased for you.

Vincent (*laughs*) Thanks, thank you. Yeah, I've finally . . .

Rachel Found something to . . . (*Beat.*) And when are you coming back, or are you . . .

Vincent Well, I'm sort of just gonna, take it . . .

Rachel Sure. Yeah. Sure. Well cheers.

Vincent What? Oh yeah. Cheers. To er . . . absent – soon to be absent . . .

Rachel Friends.

Vincent (*the drinks*) I don't think these are very good actually.

Rachel No they're not . . . great –

Vincent And. But anyway, what's, what's there to hold me here? I just thought, y'know, I mean friends . . . There's my grandmother I suppose but she'll be dead soon.

Rachel Vincent.

Vincent It's true. Y'know, There's no one.

Beat.

Rachel There's your art?

Vincent My what? Oh well, that was something that was starting to . . . happen actually. But I think it might just be the kick up the arse it, it needs. But I've got an exhibition.

Rachel Oh wow.

Vincent Yeah the café, finally . . .

Rachel They caved in.

Vincent (*searching bag for a flyer*) Yeah they caved in to grant me a . . . a swan song, and so you can come and see it and its just a few pictures and photos and . . .

Rachel Mark . . . takes photos.

Beat.

Vincent Oh yeah?

Rachel (*laughs*) Yeah, he does. He's . . . Any . . . time off or . . . weekend he's, he takes this very old and . . . obscure . . . camera and he goes and photographs . . . things, he photographs objects. Very closely and . . . very very detailed, he makes sort of miniatures, sort of close studies. Of things. (*Beat.*) Objects.

Beat.

Vincent Wow. (*Beat.*) Are they any good?

Rachel laughs.

No?

A short pause.

Rachel (*sighs*) Well, the ones I've seen are . . . great. Y'know, technically, they're very technically . . . accomplished and . . . achieved and . . . I'm, just, not, sure, if they're . . . art. There. I've been horrible about him behind his back.

Vincent No you haven't been horrible at all.

Rachel sighs.

Vincent You haven't been horrible at all, y'know. I mean, I'm not even sure if that's the right . . . question, to ask actually, y'know. 'Is this art, is that art?' I mean, how is . . . Mark?

Beat.

Rachel (*half-laughs*) Mark's . . . he's great.

Vincent Great.

Rachel No, he's very well. He's a . . . he's a rock.

Vincent A rock?

Rachel Mm-hm.

Beat.

Vincent OK.

Beat.

What kind of rock?

Rachel He, is talking about going away. Moving.

Vincent OK.

Beat.

Rachel I mean, he's never really liked . . . London and he's not too sure about the house and . . . I mean, it sounds . . . wonderful. In lots of ways, and . . .

Beat.

Thinking, thinking . . . talking about . . . having a baby.

Beat.

Vincent Wow. (*Beat.*) That's, that's . . . Yeah. (*Beat.*) And is Mark . . . keen on this?

Rachel He's very keen.

Vincent Well. Brave man.

Rachel laughs, softly.

Brave man.

Rachel It's . . .

Vincent And you must be . . . happy of . . .

Rachel Of course.

Vincent Of course.

Rachel Yeah.

A short pause.

Vincent Yeah. (*Beat.*) So . . . fuck, d'you think . . .

Rachel You can always . . .

Vincent D'you think you're gonna . . . What was that?

Rachel You can always do things . . . too fast.

Beat.

Vincent Sure. Yeah.

A short pause.

Is that what you've done, or . . .?

Rachel This was a stupid idea, I should go.

Vincent What? Why?

Rachel We need to go, now, because this is my . . . office.

Vincent Yeah, but what, yeah, but to where?

Rachel I need to go home.

Vincent Rache.

Rachel Fuck . . . off, don't fucking . . . come here and try and bulldoze your way through my . . . life and . . . Because I'm happy now, I'm happier than I ever . . . certainly than I ever was trying to nurse you into a sense of.

Vincent A sense of what? What are you saying, what the fuck is / this . . .

35

Rachel Coming and trying to bully me into being unhappy and maybe it is . . . conventional or conservative, but you can't be a fucking student all your life and you certainly can't be *you* . . . all your life, and I had to work, hard for you. It wasn't a fucking breeze and I loved you and I cared for you and I . . . hurt myself –

Vincent Anything I did back then . . . might have been terrible but I was a mess . . . then I was a fucking mess and, and you helped me and . . . that is what I always . . .

Rachel I've got a train to catch, Vincent, I've got to go home.

Vincent Come with me.

Beat.

Please.

Beat.

Because that's what I wanted to . . . That's the only thing I wanted to . . . (*Beat.*) For you to just . . . leave . . . Mark and . . . maybe leave . . . the job and . . . just to come away and . . . because it's so fucking empty. D'you know?

A short pause.

Rachel (*quietly*) I want you to go away because you're killing me, you're killing me.

A short pause.

Go . . . Go to Australia and don't come back this time.

Beat.

Could you do that?

Beat.

For me.

They are still.

36

FOUR

June.

A cemetery beside a youth club in Small Heath, Birmingham.

Amar Saleem is sitting with his earphones in. He wears quite smart jeans and a jumper, with a large jacket on top. He is seventeen. He notices Khalid Masaudi walking purposefully nearby.

Khalid is also seventeen. He has a carrier bag with him. He wears dishevelled sportswear. He was born in Kenya, but has lived in Birmingham for four years.

Amar Khalid. Khalid.

Khalid sees him – he laughs, almost grudgingly.

Khalid Look who I see now.

Amar Yes.

Khalid Amar. What you doing here?

Amar Boy, nothing.

Khalid Nothing? Come smoke a spliff with me.

Amar No, I'm busy.

Khalid What you mean, 'busy'? Look how you just wear some big jacket you know. Don't you know that in two days time yeah it's July yeah: you don't have to wear them jackets no more.

Amar Yeah, when I reach from Pakistan I feel to, put a jacket on, ennit.

Khalid Serious?

Amar Serious.

Beat.

Khalid I didn't know that you went there you know.

Amar Boy . . .

Khalid You keep secrets, ennit.

Amar Nah man. The world's bigger than . . . West Midlands or something like that.

Khalid That's true, man, You know this. I feel angry you know.

Amar Why?

Khalid (*indicating a youth centre, off*) You go to that place?

Amar Nah.

Khalid The mans in there yeah, they're some dickheads you know. You spend all your time in a youth centre that makes you a youth yeah, don't make you a man.

Amar Is it.

Khalid Believe.

Khalid is getting out a box of fried chicken.

I need to eat some chicken.

Amar Will that make you feel better?

Khalid You're sitting on someone's grave you know, that's raw.

Amar I don't think he minds.

Khalid kisses his teeth. Beat.

You still play football?

Khalid Ah?

Amar (*imitates*) Ah?

Khalid Is that a question?

Amar What d'you mean?

Khalid Is that a question though, are you actually asking me this?

Amar I dunno, yeah.

Beat.

Khalid There's one thing I wanna say to you you know.

Amar What?

Khalid Fuck you, ennit.

Amar Why you say that for?

Khalid What's-it-called, Thanks for coming ennit. Like . . . 'Yeah I'm gonna have a birthday party for my birthday now, lemme just . . . ring my friends and say to them . . . what's-it-called, come to my birthday for my birthday ennit.' And then . . . someone who I would just *like* to be there . . . Like not even *want* to be there, just *like* to be there. And you don't even reach. (*Beat.*) Furthermore I know you from thirteen years old. And so what, when I ring you now you just think, 'Oh, lemme just . . . not even answer this phone call,' or something like this. (*Beat.*) What kind a' bullshit that?

Beat.

Amar Yeah, my dad got sick.

Khalid He's always sick.

Beat.

Amar Yeah, he died you know.

Khalid (*looks at him*) Swear down?

A short pause.

You want a chip?

Pause.

You still work for your uncle?

Amar Yeah.

Beat.

Khalid Your fucking . . . stall, ennit. Selling all the junk food and the . . . kebabs.

Amar That's it.

Beat.

Khalid You see Anwar?

Amar I see him at Stratford Road.

Khalid You go to Stratford Road?

Beat.

Amar Yeah, and what?

Khalid is staring at him. Beat. Khalid laughs. Beat.

Khalid He probably takes you on trips. (*Beat.*) And says 'Yeah. This is what you gotta do.' (*Beat.*) Does he take you on trips?

Beat.

Does Hashim go there?

Amar Sometimes.

Khalid Do you like him?

Amar I like everyone.

Khalid You like everyone? (*Beat.*) Does Kepri go there?

Amar Nah.

Beat.

Khalid He goes to me, 'I'm Egyptian yeah, come to my house I give you proper Egyptian food.' I went to his house yeah, his mum gimme burger and chips.

Amar Why don't you speak English . . . properly, like? Why don't you . . . kind a' make more of a effort to use proper words. Correctly.

Beat.

Khalid Why don't I use words correctly?

Amar Yeah.

Khalid Yeah? (*Beat.*) What you mean by that?

Amar I'm asking.

Khalid Yeah, I'm asking too. I'm asking too, as well.

Amar Why don't you wash your hair?

Khalid Oh, my hair?

Amar Yeah, your hair.

Khalid Why don't you tell me this: are you a wasteman's bitch?

Amar What?

Khalid Are you a wasteman's bitch? Do you work at the job centre now?

Amar What you talking about?

Khalid Fuck you, that's what I'm talking about.

He has produced a sheet of paper.

Look at this thing where they gimme some stupid thing the other day you know. My name is Khalid Masaudi, I am seventeen years old, I believe that I am a prospective candidate . . . (*Corrects himself.*) What's-it-called. My

41

name is Khalid Masaudi, I'm seventeen years old, I believe that I have the necessary . . . qualifications . . .

Amar is laughing.

What you doing, man? Why you laughing for?

Amar That's jokes.

Khalid Are you saying that I'm a joke now?

Amar You're a time-waster.

Khalid This is what they give me, before I can fill in . . . what's-it-called . . . applications yeah, for real things. And they actually know that I don't know how to write these things you know.

Amar (*laughing*) Oi . . .

Khalid I should throw it back in her face, you ugly white bitch.

Amar Oi pass that you know pass that.

Khalid shoves it at him. Beat.

What happened to your, apprentice thing, ennit?

Khalid (*shaking his head*) Ahhh. They want me to travel far . . .

Amar Yeah?

Khalid Every day. Fucking . . . Cornwall or something like this. Not Cornwall. Leicester. (*Beat.*) But in the morning I have to take my sister to school and these things, I can't . . . be able to do that you know.

Beat.

When you go to college or you go to a job your life is actually filled up. (*Beat.*) But when you don't have a job. You just sit on your arse. Look out the window. (*Beat.*)

42

Sometimes I hate everything you know, I look out the window I hate the trees, I hate the lamp posts. I hate the people. (*Beat.*) There's too much babies in my house as well you know.

Amar (*laughs, softly*) Is it?

Khalid All making up noise. Crying.

Amar You need to get hold of a girl and just work that.

Khalid I work girls from long yeah, they're all gay.

Amar (*laughs*) How can you say that they're gay?

Khalid Even from I was small age, now I'm bored now.

Amar You get bored too easy, man.

Khalid You're the kind a' guy yeah, where . . . certain time you just think . . . 'Fuck doing this thing yeah, lemme just do this next thing.' Or something like that. (*Beat.*) But me. (*Beat.*) That's not the way that I can do things.

Amar So which way do you do things?

Khalid Me? No way.

Amar Don't be stupid, man, what you dealing with?

Khalid (*laughs, dismissively*) 'What you dealing with?'
Amar And it's not even about . . . sitting around being sorry for yourself it's about doing things.

Khalid (*half-laughs*) Don't even try this.

Amar Try what?

Khalid Politics. I don't watch politics, I just . . . move away from politics. It's because of politics that I have to come to this country, ennit. 'Oh, thank you, politics.'

Amar What d'you mean by politics?

Khalid What do I mean by politics? What do *you* mean by politics. 'Ca you just . . . live inside your head now, ennit. Internet, you don't reach, phone call, you don't reach. (*Beat.*) Cos that's what politics will actually do to you, ennit. Make you lose something and . . . make you look for something else. Little pieces of something just . . . crawling around, 'Lemme find these things.' Watch this DVD – 'OK.' Read this book – 'OK.' Repeat after me.

Amar Do you realise that things can change?

Khalid No, not me. Not me, no way, I stay the same way still.

Amar Oh yeah, you do that, don't change things up, don't go forward.

Khalid I don't wanna go forward, I wanna go backwards. To things, when they were actually better.

Amar (*indicating job centre paper*) Go backwards to them then, ennit, they'll be happy for you. They won.

Khalid Ah?

Amar They won.

   Beat.

Khalid (*laughs*) Amar. With his daddy's big house and them . . . two cars in the driveway I think *you* won. I think they didn't win over you though, ennit.

Amar Yeah I'm not talking about money you know. If you're talking about money I'm talking about bigger situations.

Khalid Did Anwar teach you to say this? You're a good boy you know, you learn to speak good now.

Amar Yeah, you're a fucking little negro who's a fucking slave.

44

A beat. Khalid picks up the empty chicken box and throws it at him. Amar doesn't move. A beat.

Khalid You say this. You say that you know. You're a dickhead. (*Beat.*) I feel to go, I'll just go. (*Beat.*) I thought that there would actually be just one thing, or maybe just one person, who would actually stay to be there. But . . . what's-it-called, nah, nah, people too busy just . . . going forward.

Beat.

So fuck you same way.

Amar So what would you say to me if I'm still here?

Beat.

Khalid What you mean 'still here'? (*Beat.*) What, have you gone?

Beat.

(*Indicates the cemetery around him.*) I would say, 'You think all these people who died yeah, you think they're happy because they changed something or they did something?' – Nah. Nah man. Dead means Dead is Dead. And from you're dead then you stay dead, and no one don't check for you nothing, for what you did, or what you was doing, or what you was trying to do.

He starts to collect his stuff together.

'Ca what's that – Writing on the headstone. You wasteman. And keep going, ennit, keep going with them plans. Cos all a' them plans, and all what you're gonna do, that's just writing on the headstone. You idiot.

Amar Come sm— (*Beat.*) Is it booda or is it herb?

Khalid Ah?

Amar Is it booda?

45

Khalid stares at him. A beat.

Come we smoke this?

A beat. Khalid starts to skin up.

Khalid I don't call it booda, I call it herb. Do I look like
a white boy?

Amar With those trainers you do.

A short pause.

Khalid So do you dream in Urdu or English now?

A short pause.

Amar What d'you call your dad? Abbah?

Khalid I call my dad wasteman, 'ca he's a wasteman.
How can you just move your whole family yeah, from
one country to a next country yeah, and when you get
there you just . . . sit down and . . . munch the leaves.
Don't leave your house. (*Beat.*) And you're still the stupid
fucking dickhead you was in the first place.

Beat.

Amar We took my dad to, Asmah. We buried him there.
(*Beat.*) That's in Pakistan. In the mountains. (*Beat.*) The
mountains there, they're not cold, though. (*Beat.*) Not at
these times.

Beat. Amar takes a drag, coughs.

Khalid You need practice, ennit.

Amar I teached you how to smoke this.

Khalid Yeah, it's true you know.

Beat.

Don't make me talk about things yeah. I get angry.

Amar I know this.

Beat. Khalid starts to laugh.

What? What?

Khalid (*singing, falteringly*) 'My . . . My old man, said be a Villa fan, I said fuck you bollocks.' Nah, what's-it-called . . .

Amar laughs.

'Gimme five pound mate, I'll watch your car for you mate.'

Amar laughs.

'You don't want it, to be missing'.

Amar That's old school behaviour, I don't watch that.

Khalid Ahh – I don't want you to say you ain't gonna smoke spliff no more. Cos I want you to smoke spliff every day. With me. Like the old days.

Amar I told you.

Khalid Come play football with me.

Amar laughs.

Cricket – long. You need to come to Small Heath Park, yeah? Meet me at my house about three o' clock, we go chicken shop, we go rob some students, then we play football.

Amar Maybe I'll come next week.

Khalid You promise?

Amar Yeah.

Khalid You swear on your life?

Amar Yeah.

Beat.

Khalid I wish you're not lying you know.

Amar I'm not lying.

Beat.

Khalid I don't like it on my own. (*Beat.*) It's boring.

Amar I'll be there.

Beat.

Khalid And when you stand on top of that hill you see the whole world sometimes ennit.

Amar Is it.

Khalid Believe.

Beat.

I feel happy you know.

FIVE

August.
A cottage in the mountains, County Down.
Anne O'Connell is sitting in an armchair, thinking. She looks as if she is trying to remember something. She is eighty-nine. She wears quite a tatty old cardigan, with a blouse and trousers.
A radio is on quietly, in the background – a local radio station hosting quite an esoteric discussion about traditional folk music.
A car can be heard approaching, from outside. She turns to the window. She tuts. She stands, and moves towards the door, walking with a stick.
A car door slams shut. We hear an inner front door opening.

Anne (*as she exits*) I spent near half an hour on the telephone last week telling you people not to call again at all.

Her voice fades as she opens the outer front door. A pause. Noises off. Anne re-enters, followed by John Cayley, who is holding his police ID card, and wearing his non-uniform uniform.

(*As she enters.*) Oh.

John Are you . . . all right there, are you?

Beat.

Are you . . . (*OK?*)

Anne Sure I've no one calling for . . . two weeks at all and I'm, I'm, thinking it's your meals-on-wheels type of feller again. But it's yourself.

Beat.

You'll be wanting a cup of tea, I suppose.

John clears his throat.

I'll disappoint you.

John May I sit down, Mrs O'Connell?

Beat.

Anne I should think you probably could, if you put your mind to it.

John half-smiles, obligingly, as he sits.

Folk can do all manner a' things . . . (*She starts to sit.*) Once they've put their minds to it.

John Will I, will I help you there, or . . .

Anne doesn't hear, as she sits. A beat.

Anne Looks like you're seeing ghosts, Inspector Cayley. (*Beat.*) Is there much time for the old ceilidh in your life is there? (*Beat.*) Or I should say you're more a man of the straight and the narrow, are you?

John Mrs O'Connell, am I right in thinking, you've a grandson? Named Vincent?

A short pause.

Anne Am I right in . . . (*Beat.*) I've two. Grandsons. (*Beat.*) I've Jamie, in Australia, and . . . and Vincent.

Beat.

John Do you / ever.

Anne Vincent lives in London now.

John Yes.

Anne For . . . oh, a long time. (*Beat.*) Has Vincent got himself in trouble now?

John This is a very . . . terrible thing to have / to.

Anne I can't hear you over there, would you bring yourself closer?

John (*doing so*) Yes. Yes. It's er . . . Do you . . . Do you follow the news? At all? Mrs O'Connell?

Beat.

Anne D'you mean the newspapers?

John Er . . .

Anne I don't take the papers at all, it's all grim and grime and . . . not worth the reading of it, I'm sure.

John It's –

Anne I'm an old woman, Inspector, would you tell me what this is about? Please?

Beat.

John I understand that Vincent, was caught up, altogether, in . . . events, that happened, last week. In London.

   Beat.

Anne Events?

John Yes.

   Beat.

Anne In London?

   Beat.

Is this what you've come to tell me? (*Beat.*) That Vincent was caught up, in events last week in London?

John There were major, incidents, that happened, and . . . many people were killed, and, and Vincent I believe was in a supermarket, in the centre of the . . . London . . .

Anne Is he dead?

   Beat.

John Yes.

   A short pause.

Anne What was the name of your man? (*Beat.*) Rugby playing feller. (*Beat.*) In the seventies.

   Beat.

He was a Galway man so he was.

John Er, Jerry Graham?

Anne Jerry Graham. I've a terrible head for remembering things these days.

John There seemed to be . . . There was trouble, I'm told, tracking Vincent down. That's to say his relatives. Was your grandson something of a nomad? D'you know?

Anne Vincent's a great and dirty mouth on him.

Beat.

John Were you in contact with him?

Anne Sometimes.

John Sometimes?

Anne Sometimes yes, sometimes no.

Beat.

John He was your daughter's son?

Beat.

Anne (*half-laughs*) Sure I'm halfway to thinking you know more of him than I do.

Beat.

He had a girlfriend. She had purple hair and a ring through her nose. And they were about . . . leaving, the university together and getting a house. (*Beat.*) But she had done with him. Married another feller. (*Beat.*) He rang me up and was all . . . (*Beat. Half-laughs.*) That he missed his mother. That he was . . . going to go and see them all. Before they all died, he said.

Beat.

John Your daughter's Katherine, Cairns?

Beat.

Anne That's the name she gained through marriage, Inspector.

Beat.

John And she lives in Australia?

Beat.

Anne I don't know that she's ever lived anywhere, always itching to be somewhere else. Always missing something.

Beat.

John She hasn't . . . asked after Vincent? Maybe wondered, why it is he hasn't . . . called? Or some such?

Beat.

Anne I haven't seen Katherine for . . . seven years. (*Beat.*) She came back for a . . . friend of hers was getting married down near Dublin, I think. But she . . . she didn't come up here for . . . I don't know. (*Beat.*) Had herself some funny ideas about . . . took herself off to England and raised the children there and then when she's taken leave of that, she says, 'We're off to Australia.' And she goes. And, and Vincent went too and, and then he came back. But he, he takes after his mother in . . . many ways and . . .

A short pause.

And there's a time, comes. (*Beat.*) And you look at your only child and you say to yourself, 'What have we here?' and there's laughter, and a kindness, and a hope. (*Beat.*) And you put these things there. (*Beat.*) But there's also selfishness. (*Beat.*) And a wanting to . . . break, smash, take. (*Beat.*) Because you put that there too. That's there, strong as the rest. (*Beat.*) She's a small and selfish child and I'll have none of it.

Beat.

John Mrs O'Connell, we need to reach Katherine. (*Beat.*) There are things, which must be done . . . And, and whatever about that, she . . . should know. Shouldn't she?

Beat.

I know this must be an awful, and a dreadful thing to have to . . . I understand that, of course.

Anne Have you any children yourself, Inspector?

Beat.

John No.

A short pause.

Anne Then could you tell me . . . (*Beat.*) Could you please tell me how, in any particular way one ounce of this could be understandable to you?

A pause.

Help me get up.

John stands and starts to help her up from her seat. She moves slowly towards an old telephone. A beat.

I've a number for the house in Sydney.

She searches through an address book before settling on a page. A beat. She takes a deep breath before slowly, painfully, dialling the number. She waits. John watches. A short pause, then –

(*On phone.*) Jamie?

A beat. She sighs.

Answering machine, of course.

She hesitates, then sighs again.

Oh . . .

She puts the receiver down and brushes the thought away with her hand.

Will you have me ring and ring till anyone or the Devil picks up?

John (*softly*) Will you cry now, will you?

Anne What?

John (*louder*) Will you cry? Why won't you cry?

A beat. She is staring at him. John seems to have surprised himself.

Anne Go on out of this house.

Beat.

John I . . .

Anne That I, was just now . . . taking you into my house . . .

John Mrs O'Connell.

Anne Go on.

John hesitates by the door. A beat.

John I'd a child once, a wee boy, and he was . . . as you say, laughter, a kindness, and, but there were two men in a car . . . (*Beat.*) And we sent him to the school in Hilltown there and in the church beside the school he was, there was . . . classes, in the church beside the school there for the . . . after-school and the painting and all this, and . . . but there were two . . . and it'd be . . . the bus back home after that. But there were two fellers in a car one time. And there was, in . . . a bomb. In the back of the car one time, and there were two men in a car and there was a bomb in the car. And they were on their way up to Belfast I think but the thing, but the bomb . . . prematurely . . . as they were passing by the bus stop there and he was at the bus stop, my son, he was waiting for the . . . (*Beat.*) He was waiting at the bus stop there.

A short pause.

I'll leave you my number at the station. (*Beat.*) And then I'll see that, a colleague can . . .

Anne I'll take no lectures from you. (*Beat.*) It's no . . .

business of anyone's as to how . . . someone's suffered this and someone that. (*Beat.*) We're all together in being alone and that's, that's . . .

A short pause.

John I never thought I'd be a policeman but I always thought I'd be a father. (*Beat.*) My name is John.

A short pause.

Anne How old are you, John?

John I'm sixty-five.

A short pause.

Anne My husband died, six months prior to his retirement date.

Beat.

And you've drawn a short straw today, Mr Cayley. Bringing yourself the way up here. Am I right?

Beat.

John It's a beautiful view you have.

Anne Aye, it was once, I suppose.

Beat.

John Mountains are fine in any weather.

Anne Aye. And your blue lady.

John laughs, softly.

Wanders about of a night apparently, looking for something lost, though I've never seen her. (*Beat.*) Perhaps I am she.

Beat.

John Came up, hereabouts, in the spring. (*Beat.*) With the old . . . paintbrush and this, d'you know?

Anne Are you a painter yourself?

John (*smiles, shaking his head*) Ah. Sure maybe I was one, nearly.

Anne Nearly?

Beat.

John Is there someone in the village, might come up and sit with you?

Anne These people in London, were they young fellers?

Beat.

John I believe so.

Beat.

Anne And why did they do these things?

Beat.

John I don't know. (*Beat.*) I think maybe there are always those who . . . would rather die than . . . carry on in the ways they're stuck.

Beat.

Anne Yes, I believe there've been times when I'd think you right.

Beat.

What was the name of your boy who was killed?

A short pause.

John It's peculiar, it's . . . a thing . . . that'd keep you awake at night but, he was called Vincent. We called him Vincent. (*Beat.*) And so hearing about . . . your grandson there, it's . . . (*Beat.*) I've thought of nothing else all morning.

Beat.

Anne Did you ever go to London, John?

Beat.

John When I was a young feller.

Anne Would you ever go back?

Beat.

John There's time and . . . all sorts between then and now.

Anne I think you should. I think there are times to surprise ourselves.

A short pause.

John (*nods, half-laughs*) Hm. (*Beat.*) This is my office number. (*Beat.*) This is my mobile. (*Beat.*) I'll have someone call you and. Altogether we can make things as easy as they . . . (*can be.*)

Beat.

Is there anyone I can call for you now?

A short pause.

Anne I knew it was only trouble soon as I saw you there.

Beat.

I suppose there's funerals and things to be thought of now. (*Beat.*) People who want telling and . . . and Vincent had pieces of himself all over the place, I'm sure, and . . . and I'm an old woman. (*Beat.*) And money . . .

A short pause.

58

And Katherine. (*Beat.*) Oh Katherine. (*Beat.*) What will
I tell her?

SIX

December
  Regents Park, London.
  Rachel Wilson enters, followed by Dennis Kessner.
  She is six months pregnant, and dressed more informally
than before.
  He is wrapped up in a jacket and scarf, and is breathing
heavily, as if in the aftermath of a panic attack.

Rachel OK?

Dennis OK. (*He laughs, briefly.*) OK.

  Beat.

Rachel Well, sit down.

Dennis (*negative*) Oh . . . really –

Rachel I think you should.

Dennis I'll be fine, just to . . . really.

  She produces a bottle of water. Beat.

Rachel (*half-laughs*) Well, I'm going to sit, so . . .

Dennis May I have, er . . . (*the water.*)

Rachel Yes, of course.

  She passes him the bottle. He drinks. A beat. He
  laughs, nervously.

Dennis What must you think of me?

Rachel How many times? Has this happened?

Dennis Oh, rarely. Today is extreme. For me.

Rachel Yes, it looked quite extreme to me.

Dennis Mmm?

Rachel I said it looked extreme, to me.

Dennis (*laughs*) Yes, the quickening. Of the throat, the heart . . . beating so . . . rapidly, so . . .

Rachel Nasty.

Dennis Very nasty. (*Beat.*) And your eyes . . . fill up and you feel perhaps you're almost . . . drowning, and then, but then . . .

A short pause.

Rachel This is my favourite park.

Dennis Oh, really?

Rachel Because it's next door to the zoo. And we used to go there when we were younger.

Dennis Oh well, I've been there several times but not for a long while –

Rachel It's happened quite a few times. Hasn't it? Your . . .

Dennis My . . . ?

Rachel These . . . attacks.

A short pause.

Dennis It's . . . A child, a boy, on the underground, just . . . (*Beat.*) Happy and laughing and he was the spitting image of course, of Christopher of course.

Rachel Oh . . .

Beat.

Dennis Christopher was so proud, to have his job. And this was snatched away. (*Beat.*) And your friend Vincent,

also . . . (Beat.) The wrong place at the wrong . . . (*Beat.*)
But did he speak to Christopher, was he served by him –
such a silly thing to think about of course –

Rachel It's important, to be honest. With ourselves.
I think.

   Beat.

Dennis Well . . . (*Beat. He laughs.*) My goodness, it's so
nice, to see you.

Rachel Yes, it's nice to see you too.

Dennis You must tell me. How you're getting along, the
both of you . . .

Rachel Well, we're fine, we're both fine . . . And the
doctors told us we're a girl, as you know.

Dennis Yes.

Rachel Which is nice, and, I'm living at my sister's . . .

Dennis OK.

Rachel In Putney . . .

Dennis Oh, Putney is a nice place.

Rachel Yeah, it's really nice. It's really nice. (*Beat.*) I don't
think it's very nice at all actually.

Dennis No?

Rachel It's full of people like me. And their people-
carriers.

Dennis (*laughs*) Yes, wonderful.

Rachel I'd like to kick them all back into the womb.

   She clears her throat. A beat.

Erm, but she's got a garden. My sister has a garden?

Dennis Uh-huh.

Rachel With a big lawn. Big . . . I think it's a big . . . Acer? Tree?

Dennis OK.

Rachel And it's very frosty. And very cold. And very quiet.

Beat.

Dennis And how long have you taken time? Off? From your workplace?

Rachel Erm, well, I've left work. (*She laughs.*) I've left work. And, so it's all a blank . . . canvas really. I mean, I didn't really expect. To have a baby. Yet. And I didn't really expect to be on my own, so . . .

Dennis And is Mark . . . in contact to . . .

Rachel Well, Mark says I treated him like a cunt. And I quote. (*Beat.*) So yeah. So we'll just have to see . . . (*how it goes.*)

Beat.

Dennis Well, always, we have always . . . expectations and . . . always there are things that we can't control, and, you know, when I think about things, and when I came to London and . . . there are many things, that I like and there are many things, which I don't like . . .

Rachel Did you come to London to teach?

Dennis Well, I came to London to play the piano.

Rachel Of course.

Dennis And to see things. To meet people. (*Beat.*) And . . . And maybe because . . . (*Beat.*) Oh perhaps because I thought I'd . . . lost something. In Germany.

Rachel You'd lost something.

Beat. He half-laughs.

Dennis And I thought I would find it in England.

A short pause.

Rachel What do you . . . ? Because of course you're freelance, so . . .

Dennis (*laughs*) Oh.

Rachel I'm interested in how you shape. Your days. Your routine.

Dennis Well, sometimes it is easy and sometimes it is very difficult to, to, to focus oneself and it's very . . . even the time of year is, er . . . important, you know, how we feel, the weather . . . I mean, I don't like Christmas, you know, I'm not a Christmas person at all, so now . . .

Rachel Yes.

Dennis It's difficult.

Rachel And is Martin coming back from . . . New York?

Dennis Martin, came back, it's too cold for him – (*he laughs*) in New York.

Rachel Oh no.

Dennis And so he's back but he's not, he's not . . . (*Beat.*) I don't know if we will ever . . . (*He nods.*)

Beat.

Rachel Is he still very angry? With the world?

Dennis Oh, he's a very angry person sometimes.

Rachel Yes, I think I'm the same.

Dennis Mmm?

Rachel I said I think I'm the same, sometimes.

Dennis (*laughs*) Oh, well, the two of you can be together then.

Rachel Yes.

Dennis You can have a boxing match or something like this. Wonderful.

   Beat.

(*With a forced casualness.*) Of course he wants to have children . . .

   Beat.

And Christopher. (*Beat.*) Christopher was very fond of him. He was very fond of him. (*Beat.*) Because, often they would accompany each other, with the piano, and the cello, and this meant a great deal to Christopher of course, he lit, lit . . . (*Beat.*) Lighted up. (*Beat.*) But, it reminds me, I need a diary, I must have a diary, because of course when you have pupils, you must . . . when, when . . . to keep track and . . . of course to keep track of, of these, er . . .

   He stops. A beat. He is trying to disguise the fact that he is crying. She moves to hold him – hesitates, then doesn't. A short pause.

Forgive me.

Rachel No, it's . . .

   Beat.

Dennis But look at you. (*Beat.*) You're so young. And you have your daughter, to come. And the two of you can do wonderful things.

Rachel Well, we'll do our best.

Dennis Well, you must do.

Rachel I wonder what she'll be like.

Dennis (*laughs*) Yes.

Rachel I worry. (*Beat.*) I mean, I'm sure I'll love her, but I hope I'll like her too. If you know what I mean.

Beat.

Dennis Well, she'll have the whole universe in front of her, and you must tell her this.

Rachel I will do.

Beat.

Dennis Because it's *now*, there's only *now*. (*Beat.*) And you don't have to change the world but you must live in it, certainly.

Beat.

Rachel I think Vincent did that, too much. (*Beat.*) He had very little sense of time. And a tiny sense of geography.

Beat.

Dennis / Do you.

Rachel The last –

Beat.

The last time I saw him I wanted to tell him, that I was, pregnant. (*Beat.*) I was going to tell him. (*Beat.*) Yeah, I don't know why I didn't do that.

A beat. She half-laughs.

I've got to go and help bury his grandmother.

Dennis half-laughs.

(*Smiling.*) So . . . Why did you laugh?

Dennis (*smiling, shaking his head*) I . . .

Rachel Did you laugh because I laughed? I'm not sure why I laughed. Erm, because his family are still over, from Australia and . . . they asked me to come and . . .

Dennis Do you, do you like them?

Rachel Well, I've only met them once, and that's when I had . . . purple hair and a ring through my nose and they didn't like that very much.

Dennis (*laughs*) Oh. Wonderful.

Rachel I was quite a different person then. I'm more like me now. I hope.

Dennis Well, of course you are, we grow into ourselves, of course.

Rachel They'll probably ask me how I am. Won't they? (*Beat.*) They'll ask me how I'm getting on. Don't you think?

    Beat.

I think I'm going to tell them I'm . . . exorbitantly happy. (*Beat.*) Yeah. (*Beat.*) And that Vincent's . . . dying was the best thing that / ever happened to me.

Dennis (*laughs uncomfortably*) Oh.

Rachel I think Vincent would appreciate that. I think he'd appreciate the honesty.

Dennis (*laughs*) The honesty . . .

Rachel I still think about him every day, but not in ways you might expect.

Dennis I . . .

Rachel I think about a lot of things. I think if I grew up in Birmingham I'd pick up a gun. Or a bomb. I mean, have you been there?

Dennis stands up.

I don't think they were cowards at all, I think how brave. How honest.

Dennis Please, may I . . .

He takes the water again. A beat.

Rachel When you went to the memorial service what did you think of it?

Dennis Er . . .

Rachel Were you embarrassed? I was embarrassed. Why did you want to talk to me, d'you think, when you first saw me?

Dennis sighs, shaking his head.

Dennis I . . . Here is someone, who is on their own, who is also bereaved, I . . .

Rachel D'you think you saw something you recognised?

Dennis We would hope there is something to recognise in all of us.

Rachel Tell me about Christopher.

Dennis Now is not the time.

Rachel I'd like to hear. Anything.

Beat.

Dennis Christopher came to me, when he was twelve years old, from the children's home, which was a place, at the time that sent me many pupils, and he came to me on Tuesdays, and then Thursdays, and . . . The family were from, originally from Nigeria but were . . . estranged . . .

Rachel What was he like?

Dennis Like? (*Laughs.*) How can we say . . . ? (*Beat.*) He was a boy who was . . . always a boy, really, because of his age, of learning, who was . . . but he played, the piano, so beautifully, you know I mean he could have been a musician . . .

Rachel Did you love him?

Dennis And he was vulnerable . . .

Rachel Did you love him?

Dennis sighs, pacing. Beat.

What are you thinking about?

Dennis Please . . .

Rachel If you were going to be honest with yourself, d'you think you'd rather have Christopher or Martin?

Dennis Be quiet, please.

Rachel When you feel like you're drowning, what are you thinking about?

Dennis Stop it.

Rachel Tell me.

He turns to her.

Dennis You think that here is someone who has not been honest? With himself? You think that when . . . the night, is . . . in the middle of the night and you're truly alone, you think I haven't been honest then? Or in the mornings or the evenings or the middle of the daytime also? (*Beat.*) I, have been honest with myself, in ways that you wouldn't . . . In ways that you would grow to hate yourself.

A short pause.

And he could never be what I wished him to be, so . . .

A short pause.

Rachel I'm sorry.

A short pause.

I suppose what hurts the most is the world insists on going on. (*Beat.*) In spite. (*Beat.*) Don't you think?

A short pause.

Dennis When I first came, to London. I had hardly any English. Only verb . . . words, and some noun . . . words. (*Beat.*) Piano. Table. (*Beat.*) Leave. Arrive. (*Beat.*) Remember. (*Beat.*) Forget.

Beat.

Rachel I wish you could be happy, but I don't know who you are.

A short pause. Rachel half-laughs.

I'm so cold.

Beat.

Dennis (*softly*) Yes.

SEVEN

July.
  The South Bank, London.
  Rachel and Vincent have ended up by the river. It is now later in the evening.
  There are various photographs laid out on the ground, that Rachel is looking at.

Vincent What an almost beautiful fucking city. You're looking at my favourite (*photo*). No that's not my favourite, that's my favourite.

69

Rachel Which?

Vincent Oh, I dunno, they're all great, they're all shite, Fuck you. Fuck you, London. Fuck you, Rachel Wilson.

Rachel (*indicating picture*) That's in Mile End.

Vincent That's the view from the old flat.

Rachel (*wistful*) Oh.

Vincent And that one's called 'The Edge'. Which was inspired by Patrick, from the café.

Rachel The edge of what?

Vincent I don't know, I think there was some comment. About, er, brinkmanship. Or some such. Which is the feeling that, we have to lead a life on the edge of some kind of pain, or in the shadow of some kind of violence to feel . . . vindicated or some sort of fucking . . . bollocks. It rang bells for me. Some time.

Rachel Right.

Beat.

Vincent The necessity of viole— He'd been mugged, y'know, and beaten quite badly and he'd found a way of . . . working it out somehow, that the violence was justified because it was the product of a valid emotion, just as valid as, as love or . . . or a more positive emotion or some . . . And so it was justifiable, just as justifiable as when his . . . grandfather . . . plied him with sweets and then buggered him when he was ten, I suppose. It's all bollocks He's a prick. He's a . . . Buddhist. D'you know?

Rachel (*the photos*) I do think they're excellent.

Vincent No, you don't. Really? (*Beat.*) I used to think you were pretty excellent. (*Beat.*) Y'know? (*Beat.*) I think we outlived the impulse that . . . bonded us. If I'm honest. Which I am. Sometimes.

She isn't looking at him.

Rachel I think about you all the time. (*Beat.*) But you're a child. (*Beat.*) And Mark . . .

A short pause.

Vincent Rache?

Beat.

Rachel I've . . . (*She shakes her head.*)

Beat.

Vincent What?

Beat.

What?

Beat.

Rachel Just . . .

A short pause.

Vincent Is it . . . I mean . . . Do you know what you want to say, and . . . you can't say it, or . . . (*Beat.*) Because it's best just to say it. I think.

Rachel half-laughs, shaking her head. A beat.

Rachel How long are you going to Australia for?

Beat.

Vincent I don't know. (*Laughs.*) I don't know.

Rachel Ten years? Twenty?

Vincent Maybe I'll come back next month.

Rachel (*laughs*) I don't know, I don't know if that would surprise me or –

Vincent I don't even know what I'm gonna. But I do feel like the windows are all wide open now, I feel that, and I can't –

Rachel is putting her head in her hands.

Listen, I can't spend my life grieving for you. (*Beat.*) Which is what I was . . . in danger of doing. Or at least for an idea of you. Was probably more accurate.

Beat.

Rachel You're a prick.

Vincent I love you.

Rachel I've . . . got a mortgage.

Vincent If I was to meet you for the first time now I'd snap you up quicker than a fucking . . . something.

Rachel But I'm sensible now.

Vincent I put half my posessions in a bag and I burnt them, did I tell you that?

Rachel Why?

Vincent I don't know.

Rachel That's, that's not good –

Vincent Don't don't don't have a baby. (*Beat.*) Don't have a baby.

Beat.

Yet. (*Beat.*) Y' know, leave it, take it slowly. Y' know. There's no rush.

Beat. Rachel half-laughs. She nods. A beat.

Rachel I should go.

Beat.

Vincent Back to Bognor.

Rachel Purley.

Vincent Slippery slope. Let me check I've got your . . . email. Shit. Fuck.

Rachel What?

Vincent I need to get a bus.

He starts collecting up the pictures.

Rachel You can get a night bus / can't you?

Vincent I get a night bus I get distracted, I end up on some . . . adventure.

Rachel Well, I'm going to London Bridge.

Vincent I'm going . . . I don't know.

Rachel Well, when will I see you again?

Vincent I don't know.

Rachel I'll come to your paintings.

Vincent Great. I might not be there.

Rachel OK. Well, thank you.

Vincent Don't worry.

Rachel No, really.

Vincent No, really. Don't worry. You know I do think you just get a bit paranoid.

Rachel Yes.

Vincent Too much.

Rachel Yes.

Vincent About everything.

Rachel I know.

Vincent You know, and maybe it sounds a bit trite.

Rachel No.

Vincent To say that, you know. People used to say it to me and I found it a bit trite but really people are only people, y'know. And no one wants to hurt you really, everyone just wants to like you. And be liked. Y' know, I really think that's true, I do. And er, and someone asked me, what I thought I'd miss the most, about London and er, and I said I thought it would be you. (*Beat.*) So there you go.

Beat.

Rachel You're going to miss your bus.

Vincent Write to me.

Rachel You write to me.

Vincent I will do.

He gives her a kiss. Beat.

I don't like saying goodbye.

Beat.

Rachel Well, let's not bother then.

Beat.

Vincent OK.

He goes. Rachel is alone.
There is a changing of the light, and sound.
Christopher comes on, and sits next to Dennis.
A piano piece echoes in the background.
Khalid comes on. He is listless. Anne comes on.
Their eyes meet.
A child's laughter echoes.

Amar and Vincent come on. They face each other.
The noises rise to a crescendo, then give way to
birdsong.

EIGHT

September.
   County Down.
   John Cayley is sitting in his back garden. His eyes are
closed, as if he is sleeping, until he opens them, suddenly.
There is noise from the house.

Margaret (*off*) Peregrines are back.

   Beat.

(*Off.*) John?

John Days are changing.

   Margaret Cayley comes out from the house. She is
   undoing her overcoat. She is sixty-four.

Margaret Swooping along all the way from town.
Goodbye, rabbit hutch.

John Goodbye, summer.

Margaret How was your day?

   Beat.

John Well, I can't remember so much, so it must've been
fine.

Margaret Misery guts. Did you take yourself to the
doctors?

John Not for headaches, woman.

Margaret But if they're coming and they're staying?

John They're coming and they're going.

A short pause.

Sullivan. Clearing his desk away.

Margaret Perhaps you'll take a leaf out of his book soon enough.

John The gold wristwatch?

Margaret shrugs at him, coyly. A beat.

I have no talent for . . . sitting at home all day.

Margaret Maybe you'll go out then.

John Maybe I will.

She exits.

Did you see I left the thing there on the table there? The leaflet there.

Margaret (*off*) The leaflet?

John There's an exhibition. Of watercolours, of the mountains.

Margaret (*off*) In town?

John In London.

Margaret (*re-entering*) London?

John 'S what I said. (*Beat.*) Might be a thing to do, maybe.

Margaret Maybe it might be.

Beat.

John Maybe you'd come with me.

She looks at him, surprised. She smiles. A beat.

Margaret Well.

She exits. A beat.

John Had your Lisa and the wee 'uns round 'bout half an hour back, I was showing them all the bunny rabbits again.

Margaret (*off*) Ah.

Beat.

John No piece of interest at all this time.

Margaret (*re-entering*) Kiddies change. Folk grow older.

John Young folk grow older.

Beat. He smiles.

We're hanging about with the lilies more than the daffodils now, you know? (*Beat.*) Sobers you up, no?

Margaret Jonathan Laurence Cayley, will I start up the violins, will I?

John Wasn't aware we had any.

Margaret Now.

She has laid out two glasses of champagne. A beat.

John What's this?

Margaret We've a celebration, haven't we?

Beat.

John?

A short pause.

Margaret (*softly*) Every year comes round and you still . . . shuffling about in the dark and keeping a lid on yourself, it might be your way, John, but it can't, it

won't . . . it can't be mine. Not now. (*Beat.*) It's not the
way he'd want it now.

Beat.

John Thought you were feigning forgotten.

Margaret Would you go on. (*Beat.*) I'll not forget.

A beat. She raises her glass.

Margaret Vincent.

John Vincent.

A short pause.

Margaret Took you five years to speak his name.

A short pause.

I'd be sitting in his room up there, with the radio on. His
'birthday songs'. (*Beat.*) And you'd be downstairs. Not
thinking of it.

John I thought of it.

A short pause.

Put your faith in this or that or say you're in love with
such and such it seems . . . a defiance, these days.

Margaret You think?

Beat.

John Tell me something about him.

Beat.

Margaret All you know is all I know.

A short pause.

John Well, there's one time. (*Beat.*) Slipped away, but . . .
came back to me when I was, up the pass up there, few
weeks back.

Margaret Which time?

Beat.

John D'you remember the old, rickety old bicycle?

Margaret (*smiles*) Yes.

John Found it round the, the back of the riding school there, I mean it was down there for weeks there, wasn't it.

Margaret I remember.

John Old-fashioned looking thing, wasn't it, with the . . . wicker basket on the front and all that. I thought, 'He won't much like the look of this,' but it was a sturdy old thing and I thought, 'Will I take it? Well I'll take it,' and I took it. And er, and he took to it well enough, didn't he?

Margaret He did.

John I thought, 'Well the lad must have some kind a' character to him to want to . . . wheel away on this old thing out a' doors without, without blushing,' d'you know?

Beat.

But no, he was . . . jumping up and down for me to let him away on it and there's a little set of wheels, been cobbled together to . . . stabilise the thing and that's, that's set him up nicely, no . . . falling off or . . . or what have you. But there's one day . . . one weekend, and I said to him in some way or other, I said it's about time to take the stabilising things off and go . . . and go off, on your own. Y'know? I said I'll take him over the tops and I'll be careful so as not to . . . let him fall and I'll be with him all the way and all this and he's, he's very much . . . not liking the idea of this at all. You know, 'Oh Dad, you mustn't let go of me,' and . . .

Beat.

But we went up, I took him up. He's on the thing there, I'm behind him, I'm holding on to the back a' the ... saddle there and ... (*Beat.*) We're going along ... faster and faster and ... he's sort of relaxing into the thing and ... I'm just sort of holding on, trying to ... bide my time and and and then I did it. I let go. (*Beat.*) And he's off. (*Beat.*) And he's away. (*Beat.*) And he's ... bumping away over the bumps and shouting and laughing and ... and I'm watching him. (*Beat.*) And he's going. (*Beat.*) And I, I just sort of thought, 'Yes, go on.' (*Beat.*) D'you know? I thought, 'Go on.' (*Beat.*) And he came up, faster and faster, up the hillside there. Laughing, echoing. (*Beat.*) And he rose up, over the ridge.

Beat.

And then he was gone.

Blackout.

The End.